FAITH. FOCUS.

A

S.M.A.R.T.

Specific. Measurable. Actionable. Relevant. Time-bound.

GOAL

DAILY PLANNER
FOR BUSINESS & LIFE

WWW.FAITHFOCUSFLOW.COM

My S.M.A.R.T. Goals Planner

Name: _____

Date: _____

Testimonials

Buying this Planner is a SMART Move!!!

I am so excited about my new planner. It is perfect for helping to set intentional action in both my business and life. As a busy professional, it is often challenging to set professional goals while keeping my personal needs in sight. This planner helps me do just that. This planner even has sections to hold you accountable for writing down your insights and lessons learned as well as your blessings. If you haven't already purchased your copy and you are serious about setting SMART goals that will actually change your life, do so today.
Amazon 5 Star Review

Attaining ALL my SMART GOALS!

I already own the book, also by TC Cooper, 52 Lessons for Christianprenuers! This planner is the perfect compliment - I am starting 2016 off right. Using Godly principles, The Word of God and now SMART goals for business and life is going to make this year a success - not only financially - but spiritually as well. I recommend this planner for any entrepreneur, student, homemaker - really anyone can use this tool for to build and attain your personal (or professional) goals!
Amazon 5 Star Review

What a difference this planner has made in my life!

What a difference this planner has made in my life. Typically, my planners have been all about places to go, people to see, things to do, but this one does that and so much more. This planner holds me accountable to myself (the tasks I outline for myself) and allows me to reflect about my inner most wishes for my purposeful life. Daily, weekly, and monthly goals are at my fingertips-- allowing for a visual reminder to myself of my personal and professional to-do lists. However, the part I enjoy most about this planner is the reminder to recommit to my personal affirmations, self-care, and my reflections of my actions. If you are looking to heighten your mindset about the way you approach personal and professional goals, this planner is for you!
Amazon 5 Star Review

I'm loving this S.M.A.R.T. Goal Daily Planner. EVERYONE NEEDS ONE OF THESE!
I fell in love the moment I opened it... I was thrilled to see a nice sized font that I don't have to strain to read and that there's plenty of room for writing. I've had other planners that forced me to write small in order to squeeze everything into a tiny space. The size and spacing of this planner is perfect!

It's important to note that the S.M.A.R.T. Goal Daily Planner is not for slackers! If you are SERIOUS about rolling up your sleeves and putting in the work, this planner will take you to task every day in creating a live blue print to achieving whatever goals you set. This is more than just writing out goals and wishing they come true... this is actually like a contract with yourself that includes a daily to-do list created by you, to keep you on track and ACCOUNTABLE. It's the holy grail for achieving goals. This planner takes you through setting goals, identifying needs and actions necessary for achieving goals, feelings and emotions evoked by the thought of accomplishing the goals, daily efforts, life balance, gratitude and rewarding yourself upon realizing your goals! The format and layout of this planner is BRILLIANT for the self motivated, disciplined, and resolved goal setter that is truly ready to accept responsibility for their own life and take action. The SMART way to reach your goals is with this planner. I'm suggesting this planner to my women's empowerment group!
Amazon 5 Star Review

Awesome Personal/Professional Project Planner!
I'm always in search of the "perfect" planner! I love this one because I'm able to personalize it to integrate short and long range projects into my busy schedule. The style is comprehensive, yet user friendly and not overwhelming. The format supports my efforts in getting clear, remaining focused, and executing each one of my personal and professional projects to completion. Perfect way to start the year.....or anytime you're ready to make those goals a reality!!
Amazon 5 Star Review

A S.M.A.R.T Goal planner is amazing!!
The S.M.A.R.T. Goal planner is an outstanding product! It's laid out in a way that makes it easy for you to get clear about your primary objective for the month, create a SMART goal for every week of the month and go through your day in a very organized manner. This formula of focusing on one SMART goal at a time is a useful way to reduce overwhelm and increase productivity. The section for monitoring your daily cash flow is also a nice touch. In addition to keeping you organized and productive, this planner will also help you reflect on what's important about each day. I highly recommend it for busy people and business owners who want to get things done.
Amazon 5 Star Review

Connect with us on social media for social marketing and business development tips on our UpwardAction channels.

Facebook:	www.Facebook.com/UpwardAction
Twitter:	www.Twitter.com/UpwardAction
Instagram:	www.Instagram.com/UpwardAction
Periscope:	www.Periscope.TV/UpwardAction

Connect with us on social media for faith based inspiration and bible-based devotionals.

Facebook:	www.Facebook.com/FaithFocusFlow
Twitter:	www.Twitter.com/FaithFocusFlow
Instagram:	www.Instagram.com/FaithFocusFlow

How To Use this S.M.A.R.T. Goal Daily Planner

ABOUT S.M.A.R.T. GOALS

This S.M.A.R.T. Goal Daily Planner helps you dream big and then make your dreams your reality, one goal at a time. This transition happens with thoughtful planning and your consistent use of S.M.A.R.T. goals. A goal becomes S.M.A.R.T. when it:

- Has a limited and narrow purpose, this makes it **<u>specific</u>** because you know exactly where to focus your attention;
- Has a clearly defined end result, this makes it **<u>measurable</u>** because you can determine when it has been accomplished;
- Is ready to be acted upon because you have or can access what is needed to accomplish it, this makes it **<u>actionable</u>** because you can do something.
- Is designed to get you closer to your vision, this makes it **<u>relevant</u>** to the big picture of your life and business.
- Has a deadline for completion, this makes it **<u>time bound</u>**.

This planner was created to help you integrate S.M.A.R.T. goals into every single area of your life. A central, special and very important part of the planner is the worksheet you complete at the beginning of every week to make your goals S.M.A.R.T. Read all about our "S.M.A.R.T. Goal Worksheet" below, then keep reading to learn about our S.M.A.R.T. system for setting your months and days up for success.

WEEKLY PLANNING ACTION:

Invest between 15 - 30 minutes at the start of every week creating at least one S.M.A.R.T. Goal related to your objective for the month.

Five (5) "S.M.A.R.T. Goal" worksheets are included for every month in the planner; one for each week and a bonus one too.

If you have multiple goals during a single week, invest in the "S.M.A.R.T. Goal" notepad at www.FaithFocusFlow.com and complete a worksheet for each of your goals.

MONTHLY PLANNING ACTION:

Invest 30-90 minutes at the start of every month completing the following steps.

Step 1.	Write down what you want to achieve within the next 12 months. Writing down your vision gives it power, so power up your vision by writing it down.	
Step 2:	Locate or draw images that bring your vision to life. Visuals inspire and invoke creativity, so inspire yourself by creating a visual of what you are working to achieve.	
Step 3:	Identify an objective for the month and commit to making it your reality during the next 4 weeks. Create an emotional connection to your objective by writing how you will feel when it is accomplished and how you will celebrate the accomplishment.	
Step 4:	Write everything needed to accomplish your objective. If you want something during the month that is not on the list, write a justification for acquiring it. This keeps you focused and within your budget.	

DAILY PLANNING ACTION:

If you invested in the 7-Day or 30-Day planner, carry it with you and use it to be intentional as you move about your day. This planner is designed for people on the move.

If you invested in the 90-Day planner, keep it on your desktop and use it to be accountable to yourself throughout your day. This planner is designed for people who primarily work in one location.

Morning:	Complete the <u>Win Every Day!</u>, <u>Today's Self-Care</u>, <u>Daily Task List</u>, and <u>Wake-Up Routine</u> sections at the start of your day to get focused on intention and achievement.	
Morning:	Select a bible verse to guide your day. Choose a different verse every day or use the same one for multiple days, weeks or months. Use the bible verse to help write a positive statement about your intention for the day. This statement is an affirmation. *Check out our "52 Lessons for Christianpreneurs" book at **www.FaithFocusFlow.com** for help in finding bible verses and creating affirmations.*	

Morning, Day and Evening	Complete the <u>Scheduled</u> column with all planned events, appointments, calls and meetings. Make note of any change to your schedule in the <u>Adjustments</u> column. Use the <u>Assessment</u> column to write down whether the scheduled item was useful or a waste of your time.	*Daily Schedule and Assessment*
Day:	Complete the <u>Contacts</u> and <u>Thank You Notes</u> section during the first half of your day. You can also do this the prior evening. Use this section to help effectively network and build relationships. Keep track of your spending and revenue in the cash columns.	*Rainmaking Relationships / Daily Task List / Today's Cash Flow*
Evening:	Complete the <u>Daily Health Check</u>, <u>Today's Lessons</u>, <u>Today's Dominate Emotion</u>, <u>Today's Blessings</u>, <u>Journaling</u>, and <u>Wind-Down Routine</u> sections at the end of your day.	*Daily Health Check / Today's Lessons / Today's Dominate Emotion / Today's Blessings / Wind-Down Routine*

Final Thoughts:

Build your life on a foundation of prayer, faith and S.M.A.R.T. goals to make your dreams your reality. There's no time to waste. Get started today.

Blessings ~
TC Cooper

Commit your
actions to the Lord,
and your plans will
succeed.

Proverbs 16:30

A Bird's Eye View of the Next 12 Months

My Vision Statement for _____.
(enter year)

In my personal life, I will:

In my business(es), I will:

At the end of the next 12 months, I will feel accomplished if:

My SMART Goal Vision Board for _____

(insert month)

Cut and paste images that represent your primary goal in the primary areas of your life *(Spirit, Health, Family Business, Fun)*. Write down a phrase to describe the goal underneath each image that you cut and paste below.

Month _____

<table>
<tr><td>This Month's Primary Objective
Every week of the month will be devoted to accomplishing this objective.</td></tr>
<tr><td></td></tr>
</table>

<table>
<tr><td align="center">How will accomplishing this goal make me feel?</td><td align="center">I will celebrate the accomplishment
of this goal by:</td></tr>
<tr><td></td><td></td></tr>
</table>

What do I need to accomplish this goal?
Complete column two by writing 'own' if you already possess the need listed, writing down the cost for acquiring the need listed or noting if the need is free. Note if the cost to acquire is one time, monthly or annual.

	Need	Do I have this or do I need to get it?
1.		
2.		
3.		
4.		
5.		
6.		
7.		
8.		
9.		
10.		

Notes

Week ONE S.M.A.R.T. Goal:

Specific:
What is the goal?

Measurable:
I will know that this goal has been accomplished when ...

Actionable:
The following are actions required to accomplish this goal. *Write the actions below and then schedule them in the following daily planning pages.*

1. _____
2. _____
3. _____
4. _____
5. _____
6. _____
7. _____
8. _____
9. _____
10. _____

Relevant:
This goal relates directly to my monthly objective because ...

Time-bound:
I will accomplish this goal no later than _____, _____ _____ at _____.
                                                     Day   Month   Date   Time

Week TWO S.M.A.R.T. Goal:

Specific:
What is the goal?

Measurable:
I will know that this goal has been accomplished when ...

Actionable:
The following are actions required to accomplish this goal. *Write the actions below and then schedule them in the following daily planning pages.*

1. _____
2. _____
3. _____
4. _____
5. _____
6. _____
7. _____
8. _____
9. _____
10. _____

Relevant:
This goal relates directly to my monthly objective because ...

Time-bound:
I will accomplish this goal no later than _____, _____ _____ at _____.
                                                          Day   **Month**   **Date**   **Time**

Week THREE S.M.A.R.T. Goal:

Specific:
What is the goal?

Measurable:
I will know that this goal has been accomplished when ...

Actionable:
The following are actions required to accomplish this goal. *Write the actions below and then schedule them in the following daily planning pages.*

1. _____
2. _____
3. _____
4. _____
5. _____
6. _____
7. _____
8. _____
9. _____
10. _____

Relevant:
This goal relates directly to my monthly objective because ...

Time-bound:
I will accomplish this goal no later than _____, _____ _____ at _____.
                                              Day   Month   Date   Time

Week FOUR S.M.A.R.T. Goal:

Specific:
What is the goal?

Measurable:
I will know that this goal has been accomplished when ...

Actionable:
The following are actions required to accomplish this goal. *Write the actions below and then schedule them in the following daily planning pages.*

1. _____
2. _____
3. _____
4. _____
5. _____
6. _____
7. _____
8. _____
9. _____
10. _____

Relevant:
This goal relates directly to my monthly objective because ...

Time-bound:
I will accomplish this goal no later than _____, _____ _____ at _____.
                                                  Day   **Month**   **Date**   **Time**

S.M.A.R.T. Goal Planner

Specific:
What is the goal?

Measurable:
I will know that this goal has been accomplished when ...

Actionable:
The following are actions required to accomplish this goal. *Write the actions below and then schedule them in the following daily planning pages.*

1. _____
2. _____
3. _____
4. _____
5. _____
6. _____
7. _____
8. _____
9. _____
10. _____

Relevant:
This goal relates directly to my monthly objective because ...

Time-bound:
I will accomplish this goal no later than _____, _____ _____ at _____.
| Day | Month | Date | Time |

If you want it and can't find it, create it. Someone else wants it too.

Use S.M.A.R.T. goals to bring the idea of it to life.

~ *TC Cooper*

My Month at a Glance

SUN	MON	TUE	WED

Month _____

THU	FRI	SAT	Notes

Day: _____

Date: _____

Win Every Day!
(Write down today's top objective.)

Goal:

My Reward:

Today's Self-Care
(Non-Negotiable)

Daily Task List

Priority Tasks

1.

2.

3.

Bonus Tasks

1.

2.

3.

Tasks to Delegate

1.

2.

3.

Today's Cash Flow

Cash In	Cash Out
Total In _____	Total Out _____

Daily Health Check
(How did I exercise my body for at least 30 minutes today? How will I do it tomorrow?)

Today's Lessons
(What did I learn today?)

1.

2.

3.

Today's Dominate Emotion
(Do I want to repeat this emotion or doesit need to improve?)

Emotion:

Why?:

Keep or Improve:

Today's Blessings
(Today I am grateful for:)

1.

2.

3.

Today's Scripture:	

Today's Affirmation:	

Wake-Up Routine

☐	Warm Water + Lemon	☐	Meditate
☐	Pray	☐	Affirm
☐	Exercise	☐	Express Love
☐	_____	☐	_____

Daily Schedule and Assessment

(In the Assessment column, write down if the actual activity that occurred was useful, wasteful or if the jury's still out.)

	Scheduled	Adjustments	Assessment
4AM			
5 AM			
6 AM			
7 AM			
8 AM			
9 AM			
10 AM			
11 AM			
12 PM			
1 PM			
2 PM			
3 PM			
4 PM			
5 PM			
6 PM			
7 PM			
8 PM			
9 PM			
10 PM			
11 PM			
12 AM			
1 AM			
2 AM			
3 AM			

Wind-Down Routine

☐	Reflect	☐	Give Thanks
☐	Plan	☐	Ask
☐	Pray	☐	Release
☐	_____	☐	_____

Journaling: Wind-Down Reflections

- Who did I help today and how?

_____

_____

_____

_____

- Who helped me today and how?

_____

_____

_____

_____

- What do I want to remember most about today?

_____

_____

_____

_____

- What do I want tomorrow to bring?

_____

_____

_____

_____

Rainmaking Relationships

People to Contact Today

Thank You Notes to Send Today

Daily Reflections

Day: _____   Date: _____

Win Every Day!
(Write down today's top objective.)

Goal:

My Reward:

Today's Self-Care
(Non-Negotiable)

Daily Task List

Priority Tasks
1.
2.
3.
Bonus Tasks
1.
2.
3.
Tasks to Delegate
1.
2.
3.

Today's Cash Flow

Cash In	Cash Out
Total In _____	Total Out _____

Daily Health Check
(How did I exercise my body for at least 30 minutes today? How will I do it tomorrow?)

Today's Lessons
(What did I learn today?)

1.
2.
3.

Today's Dominate Emotion
(Do I want to repeat this emotion or doesit need to improve?)

Emotion:

Why?:

Keep or Improve:

Today's Blessings
(Today I am grateful for:)

1.
2.
3.

Today's Scripture:	
Today's Affirmation:	

Wake-Up Routine

☐	Warm Water + Lemon	☐	Meditate
☐	Pray	☐	Affirm
☐	Exercise	☐	Express Love
☐	_____	☐	_____

Daily Schedule and Assessment
(In the Assessment column, write down if the actual activity that occurred was useful, wasteful or if the jury's still out.)

	Scheduled	Adjustments	Assessment
4AM			
5 AM			
6 AM			
7 AM			
8 AM			
9 AM			
10 AM			
11 AM			
12 PM			
1 PM			
2 PM			
3 PM			
4 PM			
5 PM			
6 PM			
7 PM			
8 PM			
9 PM			
10 PM			
11 PM			
12 AM			
1 AM			
2 AM			
3 AM			

Wind-Down Routine

☐	Reflect	☐	Give Thanks
☐	Plan	☐	Ask
☐	Pray	☐	Release
☐	_____	☐	_____

Journaling: Wind-Down Reflections

- Who did I help today and how?

_____

_____

_____

- Who helped me today and how?

_____

_____

_____

- What do I want to remember most about today?

_____

_____

_____

- What do I want tomorrow to bring?

_____

_____

_____

Rainmaking Relationships

People to Contact Today

Thank You Notes to Send Today

Daily Reflections

Day: _____   Date: _____

Win Every Day!
(Write down today's top objective.)

Goal:

My Reward:

Today's Self-Care
(Non-Negotiable)

Daily Task List

Priority Tasks
1.
2.
3.
Bonus Tasks
1.
2.
3.
Tasks to Delegate
1.
2.
3.

Today's Cash Flow

Cash In	Cash Out
Total In _____	Total Out _____

Daily Health Check
(How did I exercise my body for at least 30 minutes today? How will I do it tomorrow?)

Today's Lessons
(What did I learn today?)

1.
2.
3.

Today's Dominate Emotion
(Do I want to repeat this emotion or doesit need to improve?)

Emotion:

Why?:

Keep or Improve:

Today's Blessings
(Today I am grateful for:)

1.
2.
3.

Today's Scripture:	

Today's Affirmation:	

Wake-Up Routine

☐	Warm Water + Lemon	☐	Meditate
☐	Pray	☐	Affirm
☐	Exercise	☐	Express Love
☐	_____	☐	_____

Daily Schedule and Assessment

(In the Assessment column, write down if the actual activity that occurred was useful, wasteful or if the jury's still out.)

	Scheduled	Adjustments	Assessment
4AM			
5 AM			
6 AM			
7 AM			
8 AM			
9 AM			
10 AM			
11 AM			
12 PM			
1 PM			
2 PM			
3 PM			
4 PM			
5 PM			
6 PM			
7 PM			
8 PM			
9 PM			
10 PM			
11 PM			
12 AM			
1 AM			
2 AM			
3 AM			

Wind-Down Routine

☐	Reflect	☐	Give Thanks
☐	Plan	☐	Ask
☐	Pray	☐	Release
☐	_____	☐	_____

Journaling: Wind-Down Reflections

- Who did I help today and how?

_____

_____

_____

_____

- Who helped me today and how?

_____

_____

_____

_____

- What do I want to remember most about today?

_____

_____

_____

_____

- What do I want tomorrow to bring?

_____

_____

_____

_____

Rainmaking Relationships

People to Contact Today

Thank You Notes to Send Today

Daily Reflections

Day: _____   Date: _____

Win Every Day!
(Write down today's top objective.)

Goal:

My Reward:

Today's Self-Care
(Non-Negotiable)

Daily Task List

Priority Tasks
1.
2.
3.
Bonus Tasks
1.
2.
3.
Tasks to Delegate
1.
2.
3.

Today's Cash Flow

Cash In	Cash Out
Total In _____	Total Out _____

Daily Health Check
(How did I exercise my body for at least 30 minutes today? How will I do it tomorrow?)

Today's Lessons
(What did I learn today?)

1.
2.
3.

Today's Dominate Emotion
(Do I want to repeat this emotion or doesit need to improve?)

Emotion:

Why?:

Keep or Improve:

Today's Blessings
(Today I am grateful for:)

1.
2.
3.

Today's Scripture:	

Today's Affirmation:	

Wake-Up Routine

☐	Warm Water + Lemon	☐	Meditate
☐	Pray	☐	Affirm
☐	Exercise	☐	Express Love
☐	_____	☐	_____

Daily Schedule and Assessment
(In the Assessment column, write down if the actual activity that occurred was useful, wasteful or if the jury's still out.)

	Scheduled	Adjustments	Assessment
4AM			
5 AM			
6 AM			
7 AM			
8 AM			
9 AM			
10 AM			
11 AM			
12 PM			
1 PM			
2 PM			
3 PM			
4 PM			
5 PM			
6 PM			
7 PM			
8 PM			
9 PM			
10 PM			
11 PM			
12 AM			
1 AM			
2 AM			
3 AM			

Wind-Down Routine

☐	Reflect	☐	Give Thanks
☐	Plan	☐	Ask
☐	Pray	☐	Release
☐	_____	☐	_____

Journaling: Wind-Down Reflections

- Who did I help today and how?

_____

_____

_____

_____

- Who helped me today and how?

_____

_____

_____

_____

- What do I want to remember most about today?

_____

_____

_____

_____

- What do I want tomorrow to bring?

_____

_____

_____

_____

Rainmaking Relationships

People to Contact Today

Thank You Notes to Send Today

Daily Reflections

Day: _____   Date: _____

Win Every Day!
(Write down today's top objective.)

Goal:

My Reward:

Today's Self-Care
(Non-Negotiable)

Daily Task List

Priority Tasks

1.

2.

3.

Bonus Tasks

1.

2.

3.

Tasks to Delegate

1.

2.

3.

Today's Cash Flow

Cash In	Cash Out
Total In _____	Total Out _____

Daily Health Check
(How did I exercise my body for at least 30 minutes today? How will I do it tomorrow?)

Today's Lessons
(What did I learn today?)

1.

2.

3.

Today's Dominate Emotion
(Do I want to repeat this emotion or doesit need to improve?)

Emotion:

Why?:

Keep or Improve:

Today's Blessings
(Today I am grateful for:)

1.

2.

3.

Today's Scripture:	
Today's Affirmation:	

Wake-Up Routine

- ☐ Warm Water + Lemon
- ☐ Pray
- ☐ Exercise
- ☐ _____

- ☐ Meditate
- ☐ Affirm
- ☐ Express Love
- ☐ _____

Daily Schedule and Assessment

(In the Assessment column, write down if the actual activity that occurred was useful, wasteful or if the jury's still out.)

	Scheduled	Adjustments	Assessment
4AM			
5 AM			
6 AM			
7 AM			
8 AM			
9 AM			
10 AM			
11 AM			
12 PM			
1 PM			
2 PM			
3 PM			
4 PM			
5 PM			
6 PM			
7 PM			
8 PM			
9 PM			
10 PM			
11 PM			
12 AM			
1 AM			
2 AM			
3 AM			

Wind-Down Routine

- ☐ Reflect
- ☐ Plan
- ☐ Pray
- ☐ _____

- ☐ Give Thanks
- ☐ Ask
- ☐ Release
- ☐ _____

Journaling: Wind-Down Reflections

- Who did I help today and how?

_____

_____

_____

_____

- Who helped me today and how?

_____

_____

_____

_____

- What do I want to remember most about today?

_____

_____

_____

_____

- What do I want tomorrow to bring?

_____

_____

_____

_____

Rainmaking Relationships

People to Contact Today	Thank You Notes to Send Today

Daily Reflections

Day: _____   Date: _____

Win Every Day!
(Write down today's top objective.)

Goal:

My Reward:

Today's Self-Care
(Non-Negotiable)

Daily Task List

Priority Tasks
1.
2.
3.
Bonus Tasks
1.
2.
3.
Tasks to Delegate
1.
2.
3.

Today's Cash Flow

Cash In	Cash Out

Total In _____   Total Out _____

Daily Health Check
(How did I exercise my body for at least 30 minutes today? How will I do it tomorrow?)

Today's Lessons
(What did I learn today?)

1.
2.
3.

Today's Dominate Emotion
(Do I want to repeat this emotion or doesit need to improve?)

Emotion:

Why?:

Keep or Improve:

Today's Blessings
(Today I am grateful for:)

1.
2.
3.

Today's Scripture:	
Today's Affirmation:	

Wake-Up Routine

☐	Warm Water + Lemon	☐	Meditate
☐	Pray	☐	Affirm
☐	Exercise	☐	Express Love
☐	_____	☐	_____

Daily Schedule and Assessment

(In the Assessment column, write down if the actual activity that occurred was useful, wasteful or if the jury's still out.)

	Scheduled	Adjustments	Assessment
4AM			
5 AM			
6 AM			
7 AM			
8 AM			
9 AM			
10 AM			
11 AM			
12 PM			
1 PM			
2 PM			
3 PM			
4 PM			
5 PM			
6 PM			
7 PM			
8 PM			
9 PM			
10 PM			
11 PM			
12 AM			
1 AM			
2 AM			
3 AM			

Wind-Down Routine

☐	Reflect	☐	Give Thanks
☐	Plan	☐	Ask
☐	Pray	☐	Release
☐	_____	☐	_____

Journaling: Wind-Down Reflections

- Who did I help today and how?

_____

_____

_____

_____

- Who helped me today and how?

_____

_____

_____

_____

- What do I want to remember most about today?

_____

_____

_____

_____

- What do I want tomorrow to bring?

_____

_____

_____

_____

Rainmaking Relationships

People to Contact Today	Thank You Notes to Send Today

Daily Reflections

Day: _____   Date: _____

Win Every Day!
(Write down today's top objective.)

Goal:

My Reward:

Today's Self-Care
(Non-Negotiable)

Daily Task List

Priority Tasks
1.
2.
3.
Bonus Tasks
1.
2.
3.
Tasks to Delegate
1.
2.
3.

Today's Cash Flow

Cash In	Cash Out
Total In _____	Total Out _____

Daily Health Check
(How did I exercise my body for at least 30 minutes today? How will I do it tomorrow?)

Today's Lessons
(What did I learn today?)

1.
2.
3.

Today's Dominate Emotion
(Do I want to repeat this emotion or doesit need to improve?)

Emotion:

Why?:

Keep or Improve:

Today's Blessings
(Today I am grateful for:)

1.
2.
3.

Today's Scripture:	

Today's Affirmation:	

Wake-Up Routine

☐	Warm Water + Lemon	☐	Meditate
☐	Pray	☐	Affirm
☐	Exercise	☐	Express Love
☐	_____	☐	_____

Daily Schedule and Assessment

(In the Assessment column, write down if the actual activity that occurred was useful, wasteful or if the jury's still out.)

	Scheduled	Adjustments	Assessment
4AM			
5 AM			
6 AM			
7 AM			
8 AM			
9 AM			
10 AM			
11 AM			
12 PM			
1 PM			
2 PM			
3 PM			
4 PM			
5 PM			
6 PM			
7 PM			
8 PM			
9 PM			
10 PM			
11 PM			
12 AM			
1 AM			
2 AM			
3 AM			

Wind-Down Routine

☐	Reflect	☐	Give Thanks
☐	Plan	☐	Ask
☐	Pray	☐	Release
☐	_____	☐	_____

Journaling: Wind-Down Reflections

- Who did I help today and how?

_____

_____

_____

_____

- Who helped me today and how?

_____

_____

_____

_____

- What do I want to remember most about today?

_____

_____

_____

_____

- What do I want tomorrow to bring?

_____

_____

_____

_____

Rainmaking Relationships

People to Contact Today

Thank You Notes to Send Today

Daily Reflections

Day: _____   Date: _____

Win Every Day!
(Write down today's top objective.)

Goal:

My Reward:

Today's Self-Care
(Non-Negotiable)

Daily Task List

Priority Tasks
1.
2.
3.
Bonus Tasks
1.
2.
3.
Tasks to Delegate
1.
2.
3.

Today's Cash Flow

Cash In	Cash Out
Total In _____	Total Out _____

Daily Health Check
(How did I exercise my body for at least 30 minutes today? How will I do it tomorrow?)

Today's Lessons
(What did I learn today?)

1.
2.
3.

Today's Dominate Emotion
(Do I want to repeat this emotion or doesit need to improve?)

Emotion:

Why?:

Keep or Improve:

Today's Blessings
(Today I am grateful for:)

1.
2.
3.

Today's Scripture:	

Today's Affirmation:	

Wake-Up Routine

- ☐ Warm Water + Lemon
- ☐ Pray
- ☐ Exercise
- ☐ _____

- ☐ Meditate
- ☐ Affirm
- ☐ Express Love
- ☐ _____

Daily Schedule and Assessment

(In the Assessment column, write down if the actual activity that occurred was useful, wasteful or if the jury's still out.)

	Scheduled	Adjustments	Assessment
4AM			
5 AM			
6 AM			
7 AM			
8 AM			
9 AM			
10 AM			
11 AM			
12 PM			
1 PM			
2 PM			
3 PM			
4 PM			
5 PM			
6 PM			
7 PM			
8 PM			
9 PM			
10 PM			
11 PM			
12 AM			
1 AM			
2 AM			
3 AM			

Wind-Down Routine

- ☐ Reflect
- ☐ Plan
- ☐ Pray
- ☐ _____

- ☐ Give Thanks
- ☐ Ask
- ☐ Release
- ☐ _____

Journaling: Wind-Down Reflections

- Who did I help today and how?

_____

_____

_____

- Who helped me today and how?

_____

_____

_____

- What do I want to remember most about today?

_____

_____

_____

- What do I want tomorrow to bring?

_____

_____

_____

Rainmaking Relationships

People to Contact Today

Thank You Notes to Send Today

Daily Reflections

Day: _____   Date: _____

Win Every Day!
(Write down today's top objective.)

Goal:

My Reward:

Today's Self-Care
(Non-Negotiable)

Daily Task List

Priority Tasks
1.
2.
3.
Bonus Tasks
1.
2.
3.
Tasks to Delegate
1.
2.
3.

Today's Cash Flow

Cash In	Cash Out
Total In _____	Total Out _____

Daily Health Check
(How did I exercise my body for at least 30 minutes today? How will I do it tomorrow?)

Today's Lessons
(What did I learn today?)

1.
2.
3.

Today's Dominate Emotion
(Do I want to repeat this emotion or doesit need to improve?)

Emotion:

Why?:

Keep or Improve:

Today's Blessings
(Today I am grateful for:)

1.
2.
3.

Today's Scripture:	

Today's Affirmation:	

Wake-Up Routine

☐	Warm Water + Lemon	☐	Meditate
☐	Pray	☐	Affirm
☐	Exercise	☐	Express Love
☐	_____	☐	_____

Daily Schedule and Assessment

(In the Assessment column, write down if the actual activity that occurred was useful, wasteful or if the jury's still out.)

	Scheduled	Adjustments	Assessment
4AM			
5 AM			
6 AM			
7 AM			
8 AM			
9 AM			
10 AM			
11 AM			
12 PM			
1 PM			
2 PM			
3 PM			
4 PM			
5 PM			
6 PM			
7 PM			
8 PM			
9 PM			
10 PM			
11 PM			
12 AM			
1 AM			
2 AM			
3 AM			

Wind-Down Routine

☐	Reflect	☐	Give Thanks
☐	Plan	☐	Ask
☐	Pray	☐	Release
☐	_____	☐	_____

Journaling: Wind-Down Reflections

- Who did I help today and how?

_____

_____

_____

_____

- Who helped me today and how?

_____

_____

_____

_____

- What do I want to remember most about today?

_____

_____

_____

_____

- What do I want tomorrow to bring?

_____

_____

_____

_____

Rainmaking Relationships

People to Contact Today	Thank You Notes to Send Today

Daily Reflections

Day: _____   Date: _____

Win Every Day!
(Write down today's top objective.)

Goal:

My Reward:

Today's Self-Care
(Non-Negotiable)

Daily Task List

Priority Tasks
1.
2.
3.
Bonus Tasks
1.
2.
3.
Tasks to Delegate
1.
2.
3.

Today's Cash Flow

Cash In	Cash Out

Total In _____   Total Out _____

Daily Health Check
(How did I exercise my body for at least 30 minutes today? How will I do it tomorrow?)

Today's Lessons
(What did I learn today?)

1.
2.
3.

Today's Dominate Emotion
(Do I want to repeat this emotion or doesit need to improve?)

Emotion:

Why?:

Keep or Improve:

Today's Blessings
(Today I am grateful for:)

1.
2.
3.

Today's Scripture:			
Today's Affirmation:			

Wake-Up Routine

☐ Warm Water + Lemon	☐ Meditate
☐ Pray	☐ Affirm
☐ Exercise	☐ Express Love
☐ _____	☐ _____

Daily Schedule and Assessment
(In the Assessment column, write down if the actual activity that occurred was useful, wasteful or if the jury's still out.)

	Scheduled	Adjustments	Assessment
4AM			
5 AM			
6 AM			
7 AM			
8 AM			
9 AM			
10 AM			
11 AM			
12 PM			
1 PM			
2 PM			
3 PM			
4 PM			
5 PM			
6 PM			
7 PM			
8 PM			
9 PM			
10 PM			
11 PM			
12 AM			
1 AM			
2 AM			
3 AM			

Wind-Down Routine

☐ Reflect	☐ Give Thanks
☐ Plan	☐ Ask
☐ Pray	☐ Release
☐ _____	☐ _____

Journaling: Wind-Down Reflections

- Who did I help today and how?

_____

_____

_____

_____

- Who helped me today and how?

_____

_____

_____

_____

- What do I want to remember most about today?

_____

_____

_____

_____

- What do I want tomorrow to bring?

_____

_____

_____

_____

Rainmaking Relationships

People to Contact Today

Thank You Notes to Send Today

Daily Reflections

Day: _____   Date: _____

Win Every Day!
(Write down today's top objective.)

Goal:

My Reward:

Today's Self-Care
(Non-Negotiable)

Daily Task List

Priority Tasks
1.
2.
3.
Bonus Tasks
1.
2.
3.
Tasks to Delegate
1.
2.
3.

Today's Cash Flow

Cash In	Cash Out
Total In _____	Total Out _____

Daily Health Check
(How did I exercise my body for at least 30 minutes today? How will I do it tomorrow?)

Today's Lessons
(What did I learn today?)

1.
2.
3.

Today's Dominate Emotion
(Do I want to repeat this emotion or doesit need to improve?)

Emotion:

Why?:

Keep or Improve:

Today's Blessings
(Today I am grateful for:)

1.
2.
3.

	Today's Scripture:	

	Today's Affirmation:	

Wake-Up Routine

☐	Warm Water + Lemon	☐	Meditate
☐	Pray	☐	Affirm
☐	Exercise	☐	Express Love
☐	_____	☐	_____

Daily Schedule and Assessment
(In the Assessment column, write down if the actual activity that occurred was useful, wasteful or if the jury's still out.)

	Scheduled	Adjustments	Assessment
4AM			
5 AM			
6 AM			
7 AM			
8 AM			
9 AM			
10 AM			
11 AM			
12 PM			
1 PM			
2 PM			
3 PM			
4 PM			
5 PM			
6 PM			
7 PM			
8 PM			
9 PM			
10 PM			
11 PM			
12 AM			
1 AM			
2 AM			
3 AM			

Wind-Down Routine

☐	Reflect	☐	Give Thanks
☐	Plan	☐	Ask
☐	Pray	☐	Release
☐	_____	☐	_____

Journaling: Wind-Down Reflections

- Who did I help today and how?

_____

_____

_____

_____

- Who helped me today and how?

_____

_____

_____

_____

- What do I want to remember most about today?

_____

_____

_____

_____

- What do I want tomorrow to bring?

_____

_____

_____

_____

Rainmaking Relationships

People to Contact Today	Thank You Notes to Send Today

Daily Reflections

Day: _____   Date: _____

Win Every Day!
(Write down today's top objective.)

Goal:

My Reward:

Today's Self-Care
(Non-Negotiable)

Daily Task List

Priority Tasks
1.
2.
3.
Bonus Tasks
1.
2.
3.
Tasks to Delegate
1.
2.
3.

Today's Cash Flow

Cash In	Cash Out
Total In _____	Total Out _____

Daily Health Check
(How did I exercise my body for at least 30 minutes today? How will I do it tomorrow?)

Today's Lessons
(What did I learn today?)

1.
2.
3.

Today's Dominate Emotion
(Do I want to repeat this emotion or doesit need to improve?)

Emotion:

Why?:

Keep or Improve:

Today's Blessings
(Today I am grateful for:)

1.
2.
3.

Today's Scripture:	
Today's Affirmation:	

Wake-Up Routine

☐	Warm Water + Lemon	☐	Meditate
☐	Pray	☐	Affirm
☐	Exercise	☐	Express Love
☐	_____	☐	_____

Daily Schedule and Assessment

(In the Assessment column, write down if the actual activity that occurred was useful, wasteful or if the jury's still out.)

	Scheduled	Adjustments	Assessment
4AM			
5 AM			
6 AM			
7 AM			
8 AM			
9 AM			
10 AM			
11 AM			
12 PM			
1 PM			
2 PM			
3 PM			
4 PM			
5 PM			
6 PM			
7 PM			
8 PM			
9 PM			
10 PM			
11 PM			
12 AM			
1 AM			
2 AM			
3 AM			

Wind-Down Routine

☐	Reflect	☐	Give Thanks
☐	Plan	☐	Ask
☐	Pray	☐	Release
☐	_____	☐	_____

Journaling: Wind-Down Reflections

- Who did I help today and how?

_____

_____

_____

_____

- Who helped me today and how?

_____

_____

_____

_____

- What do I want to remember most about today?

_____

_____

_____

_____

- What do I want tomorrow to bring?

_____

_____

_____

_____

Rainmaking Relationships

People to Contact Today

Thank You Notes to Send Today

Daily Reflections

Day: _____ Date: _____

Win Every Day!
(Write down today's top objective.)

Goal:

My Reward:

Today's Self-Care
(Non-Negotiable)

Daily Task List

Priority Tasks
1.
2.
3.
Bonus Tasks
1.
2.
3.
Tasks to Delegate
1.
2.
3.

Today's Cash Flow

Cash In	Cash Out
Total In _____	Total Out _____

Daily Health Check
(How did I exercise my body for at least 30 minutes today? How will I do it tomorrow?)

Today's Lessons
(What did I learn today?)

1.
2.
3.

Today's Dominate Emotion
(Do I want to repeat this emotion or doesit need to improve?)

Emotion:

Why?:

Keep or Improve:

Today's Blessings
(Today I am grateful for:)

1.
2.
3.

Today's Scripture:	
Today's Affirmation:	

Wake-Up Routine

☐	Warm Water + Lemon	☐	Meditate
☐	Pray	☐	Affirm
☐	Exercise	☐	Express Love
☐	_____	☐	_____

Daily Schedule and Assessment

(In the Assessment column, write down if the actual activity that occurred was useful, wasteful or if the jury's still out.)

	Scheduled	Adjustments	Assessment
4AM			
5 AM			
6 AM			
7 AM			
8 AM			
9 AM			
10 AM			
11 AM			
12 PM			
1 PM			
2 PM			
3 PM			
4 PM			
5 PM			
6 PM			
7 PM			
8 PM			
9 PM			
10 PM			
11 PM			
12 AM			
1 AM			
2 AM			
3 AM			

Wind-Down Routine

☐	Reflect	☐	Give Thanks
☐	Plan	☐	Ask
☐	Pray	☐	Release
☐	_____	☐	_____

Journaling: Wind-Down Reflections

- Who did I help today and how?

_____

_____

_____

_____

- Who helped me today and how?

_____

_____

_____

_____

- What do I want to remember most about today?

_____

_____

_____

_____

- What do I want tomorrow to bring?

_____

_____

_____

_____

Rainmaking Relationships

People to Contact Today	Thank You Notes to Send Today

Daily Reflections

Day: _____   Date: _____

Win Every Day!
(Write down today's top objective.)

Goal:

My Reward:

Today's Self-Care
(Non-Negotiable)

Daily Task List

Priority Tasks
1.
2.
3.
Bonus Tasks
1.
2.
3.
Tasks to Delegate
1.
2.
3.

Today's Cash Flow

Cash In	Cash Out
Total In _____	Total Out _____

Daily Health Check
(How did I exercise my body for at least 30 minutes today? How will I do it tomorrow?)

Today's Lessons
(What did I learn today?)

1.
2.
3.

Today's Dominate Emotion
(Do I want to repeat this emotion or doesit need to improve?)

Emotion:

Why?:

Keep or Improve:

Today's Blessings
(Today I am grateful for:)

1.
2.
3.

	Today's Scripture:	
	Today's Affirmation:	

Wake-Up Routine

☐	Warm Water + Lemon	☐	Meditate
☐	Pray	☐	Affirm
☐	Exercise	☐	Express Love
☐	_____	☐	_____

Daily Schedule and Assessment

(In the Assessment column, write down if the actual activity that occurred was useful, wasteful or if the jury's still out.)

	Scheduled	Adjustments	Assessment
4AM			
5 AM			
6 AM			
7 AM			
8 AM			
9 AM			
10 AM			
11 AM			
12 PM			
1 PM			
2 PM			
3 PM			
4 PM			
5 PM			
6 PM			
7 PM			
8 PM			
9 PM			
10 PM			
11 PM			
12 AM			
1 AM			
2 AM			
3 AM			

Wind-Down Routine

☐	Reflect	☐	Give Thanks
☐	Plan	☐	Ask
☐	Pray	☐	Release
☐	_____	☐	_____

Journaling: Wind-Down Reflections

- Who did I help today and how?

_____

_____

_____

_____

- Who helped me today and how?

_____

_____

_____

_____

- What do I want to remember most about today?

_____

_____

_____

_____

- What do I want tomorrow to bring?

_____

_____

_____

_____

Rainmaking Relationships

People to Contact Today

Thank You Notes to Send Today

Daily Reflections

Day: _____   Date: _____

Win Every Day!
(Write down today's top objective.)

Goal:

My Reward:

Today's Self-Care
(Non-Negotiable)

Daily Task List

Priority Tasks
1.
2.
3.
Bonus Tasks
1.
2.
3.
Tasks to Delegate
1.
2.
3.

Today's Cash Flow

Cash In	Cash Out
Total In _____	Total Out _____

Daily Health Check
(How did I exercise my body for at least 30 minutes today? How will I do it tomorrow?)

Today's Lessons
(What did I learn today?)

1.
2.
3.

Today's Dominate Emotion
(Do I want to repeat this emotion or doesit need to improve?)

Emotion:

Why?:

Keep or Improve:

Today's Blessings
(Today I am grateful for:)

1.
2.
3.

© 2016 UpwardAction LLC
www.FaithFocusFlow.com

Today's Scripture:	
Today's Affirmation:	

Wake-Up Routine

☐	Warm Water + Lemon	☐	Meditate
☐	Pray	☐	Affirm
☐	Exercise	☐	Express Love
☐	_____	☐	_____

Daily Schedule and Assessment

(In the Assessment column, write down if the actual activity that occurred was useful, wasteful or if the jury's still out.)

	Scheduled	Adjustments	Assessment
4AM			
5 AM			
6 AM			
7 AM			
8 AM			
9 AM			
10 AM			
11 AM			
12 PM			
1 PM			
2 PM			
3 PM			
4 PM			
5 PM			
6 PM			
7 PM			
8 PM			
9 PM			
10 PM			
11 PM			
12 AM			
1 AM			
2 AM			
3 AM			

Wind-Down Routine

☐	Reflect	☐	Give Thanks
☐	Plan	☐	Ask
☐	Pray	☐	Release
☐	_____	☐	_____

Journaling: Wind-Down Reflections

- Who did I help today and how?

_____

_____

_____

_____

- Who helped me today and how?

_____

_____

_____

_____

- What do I want to remember most about today?

_____

_____

_____

_____

- What do I want tomorrow to bring?

_____

_____

_____

_____

Rainmaking Relationships

People to Contact Today	Thank You Notes to Send Today

Daily Reflections

Day: _____   Date: _____

Win Every Day!
(Write down today's top objective.)

Goal:

My Reward:

Today's Self-Care
(Non-Negotiable)

Daily Task List

Priority Tasks
1.
2.
3.
Bonus Tasks
1.
2.
3.
Tasks to Delegate
1.
2.
3.

Today's Cash Flow

Cash In	Cash Out

Total In _____   Total Out _____

Daily Health Check
(How did I exercise my body for at least 30 minutes today? How will I do it tomorrow?)

Today's Lessons
(What did I learn today?)

1.
2.
3.

Today's Dominate Emotion
(Do I want to repeat this emotion or doesit need to improve?)

Emotion:

Why?:

Keep or Improve:

Today's Blessings
(Today I am grateful for:)

1.
2.
3.

Today's Scripture:	
Today's Affirmation:	

Wake-Up Routine

☐	Warm Water + Lemon	☐	Meditate
☐	Pray	☐	Affirm
☐	Exercise	☐	Express Love
☐	_____	☐	_____

Daily Schedule and Assessment
(In the Assessment column, write down if the actual activity that occurred was useful, wasteful or if the jury's still out.)

	Scheduled	Adjustments	Assessment
4AM			
5 AM			
6 AM			
7 AM			
8 AM			
9 AM			
10 AM			
11 AM			
12 PM			
1 PM			
2 PM			
3 PM			
4 PM			
5 PM			
6 PM			
7 PM			
8 PM			
9 PM			
10 PM			
11 PM			
12 AM			
1 AM			
2 AM			
3 AM			

Wind-Down Routine

☐	Reflect	☐	Give Thanks
☐	Plan	☐	Ask
☐	Pray	☐	Release
☐	_____	☐	_____

Journaling: Wind-Down Reflections

- Who did I help today and how?

_____

_____

_____

_____

- Who helped me today and how?

_____

_____

_____

_____

- What do I want to remember most about today?

_____

_____

_____

_____

- What do I want tomorrow to bring?

_____

_____

_____

_____

Rainmaking Relationships

People to Contact Today

Thank You Notes to Send Today

Daily Reflections

Day: _____   Date: _____

Win Every Day!
(Write down today's top objective.)

Goal:

My Reward:

Today's Self-Care
(Non-Negotiable)

Daily Task List

Priority Tasks
1.
2.
3.
Bonus Tasks
1.
2.
3.
Tasks to Delegate
1.
2.
3.

Today's Cash Flow

Cash In	Cash Out
Total In _____	Total Out _____

Daily Health Check
(How did I exercise my body for at least 30 minutes today? How will I do it tomorrow?)

Today's Lessons
(What did I learn today?)

1.
2.
3.

Today's Dominate Emotion
(Do I want to repeat this emotion or doesit need to improve?)

Emotion:

Why?:

Keep or Improve:

Today's Blessings
(Today I am grateful for:)

1.
2.
3.

Today's Scripture:	

Today's Affirmation:	

Wake-Up Routine

☐	Warm Water + Lemon	☐	Meditate
☐	Pray	☐	Affirm
☐	Exercise	☐	Express Love
☐	_____	☐	_____

Daily Schedule and Assessment
(In the Assessment column, write down if the actual activity that occurred was useful, wasteful or if the jury's still out.)

	Scheduled	Adjustments	Assessment
4AM			
5 AM			
6 AM			
7 AM			
8 AM			
9 AM			
10 AM			
11 AM			
12 PM			
1 PM			
2 PM			
3 PM			
4 PM			
5 PM			
6 PM			
7 PM			
8 PM			
9 PM			
10 PM			
11 PM			
12 AM			
1 AM			
2 AM			
3 AM			

Wind-Down Routine

☐	Reflect	☐	Give Thanks
☐	Plan	☐	Ask
☐	Pray	☐	Release
☐	_____	☐	_____

Journaling: Wind-Down Reflections

- Who did I help today and how?

_____

_____

_____

_____

- Who helped me today and how?

_____

_____

_____

_____

- What do I want to remember most about today?

_____

_____

_____

_____

- What do I want tomorrow to bring?

_____

_____

_____

_____

Rainmaking Relationships

People to Contact Today

Thank You Notes to Send Today

Daily Reflections

Day: _____   Date: _____

Win Every Day!
(Write down today's top objective.)

Goal:

My Reward:

Today's Self-Care
(Non-Negotiable)

Daily Task List

Priority Tasks
1.
2.
3.
Bonus Tasks
1.
2.
3.
Tasks to Delegate
1.
2.
3.

Today's Cash Flow

Cash In	Cash Out
Total In _____	Total Out _____

Daily Health Check
(How did I exercise my body for at least 30 minutes today? How will I do it tomorrow?)

Today's Lessons
(What did I learn today?)

1.
2.
3.

Today's Dominate Emotion
(Do I want to repeat this emotion or doesit need to improve?)

Emotion:

Why?:

Keep or Improve:

Today's Blessings
(Today I am grateful for:)

1.
2.
3.

Today's Scripture:	
Today's Affirmation:	

Wake-Up Routine

☐	Warm Water + Lemon	☐	Meditate
☐	Pray	☐	Affirm
☐	Exercise	☐	Express Love
☐	_____	☐	_____

Daily Schedule and Assessment

(In the Assessment column, write down if the actual activity that occurred was useful, wasteful or if the jury's still out.)

	Scheduled	Adjustments	Assessment
4AM			
5 AM			
6 AM			
7 AM			
8 AM			
9 AM			
10 AM			
11 AM			
12 PM			
1 PM			
2 PM			
3 PM			
4 PM			
5 PM			
6 PM			
7 PM			
8 PM			
9 PM			
10 PM			
11 PM			
12 AM			
1 AM			
2 AM			
3 AM			

Wind-Down Routine

☐	Reflect	☐	Give Thanks
☐	Plan	☐	Ask
☐	Pray	☐	Release
☐	_____	☐	_____

Journaling: Wind-Down Reflections

- Who did I help today and how?

_____

_____

_____

_____

- Who helped me today and how?

_____

_____

_____

_____

- What do I want to remember most about today?

_____

_____

_____

_____

- What do I want tomorrow to bring?

_____

_____

_____

_____

Rainmaking Relationships

People to Contact Today

Thank You Notes to Send Today

Daily Reflections

Day: _____   Date: _____

Win Every Day!
(Write down today's top objective.)

Goal:

My Reward:

Today's Self-Care
(Non-Negotiable)

Daily Task List

Priority Tasks
1.
2.
3.
Bonus Tasks
1.
2.
3.
Tasks to Delegate
1.
2.
3.

Today's Cash Flow

Cash In	Cash Out
Total In _____	Total Out _____

Daily Health Check
(How did I exercise my body for at least 30 minutes today? How will I do it tomorrow?)

Today's Lessons
(What did I learn today?)

1.
2.
3.

Today's Dominate Emotion
(Do I want to repeat this emotion or doesit need to improve?)

Emotion:

Why?:

Keep or Improve:

Today's Blessings
(Today I am grateful for:)

1.
2.
3.

Today's Scripture:	

Today's Affirmation:	

Wake-Up Routine

☐	Warm Water + Lemon	☐	Meditate
☐	Pray	☐	Affirm
☐	Exercise	☐	Express Love
☐	_____	☐	_____

Daily Schedule and Assessment

(In the Assessment column, write down if the actual activity that occurred was useful, wasteful or if the jury's still out.)

	Scheduled	Adjustments	Assessment
4AM			
5 AM			
6 AM			
7 AM			
8 AM			
9 AM			
10 AM			
11 AM			
12 PM			
1 PM			
2 PM			
3 PM			
4 PM			
5 PM			
6 PM			
7 PM			
8 PM			
9 PM			
10 PM			
11 PM			
12 AM			
1 AM			
2 AM			
3 AM			

Wind-Down Routine

☐	Reflect	☐	Give Thanks
☐	Plan	☐	Ask
☐	Pray	☐	Release
☐	_____	☐	_____

Journaling: Wind-Down Reflections

- Who did I help today and how?

_____

_____

_____

_____

- Who helped me today and how?

_____

_____

_____

_____

- What do I want to remember most about today?

_____

_____

_____

_____

- What do I want tomorrow to bring?

_____

_____

_____

_____

Rainmaking Relationships

People to Contact Today

Thank You Notes to Send Today

Daily Reflections

Day: _____   Date: _____

Win Every Day!
(Write down today's top objective.)

Goal:

My Reward:

Today's Self-Care
(Non-Negotiable)

Daily Task List

Priority Tasks
1.
2.
3.
Bonus Tasks
1.
2.
3.
Tasks to Delegate
1.
2.
3.

Today's Cash Flow

Cash In	Cash Out
Total In _____	Total Out _____

Daily Health Check
(How did I exercise my body for at least 30 minutes today? How will I do it tomorrow?)

Today's Lessons
(What did I learn today?)

1.
2.
3.

Today's Dominate Emotion
(Do I want to repeat this emotion or doesit need to improve?)

Emotion:

Why?:

Keep or Improve:

Today's Blessings
(Today I am grateful for:)

1.
2.
3.

Today's Scripture:	
Today's Affirmation:	

Wake-Up Routine

☐ Warm Water + Lemon   ☐ Meditate
☐ Pray   ☐ Affirm
☐ Exercise   ☐ Express Love
☐ _____   ☐ _____

Daily Schedule and Assessment

(In the Assessment column, write down if the actual activity that occurred was useful, wasteful or if the jury's still out.)

	Scheduled	Adjustments	Assessment
4AM			
5 AM			
6 AM			
7 AM			
8 AM			
9 AM			
10 AM			
11 AM			
12 PM			
1 PM			
2 PM			
3 PM			
4 PM			
5 PM			
6 PM			
7 PM			
8 PM			
9 PM			
10 PM			
11 PM			
12 AM			
1 AM			
2 AM			
3 AM			

Wind-Down Routine

☐ Reflect   ☐ Give Thanks
☐ Plan   ☐ Ask
☐ Pray   ☐ Release
☐ _____   ☐ _____

Journaling: Wind-Down Reflections

- Who did I help today and how?

_____

_____

_____

_____

- Who helped me today and how?

_____

_____

_____

_____

- What do I want to remember most about today?

_____

_____

_____

_____

- What do I want tomorrow to bring?

_____

_____

_____

_____

Rainmaking Relationships

People to Contact Today	Thank You Notes to Send Today

Daily Reflections

Day: _____   Date: _____

Win Every Day!
(Write down today's top objective.)

Goal:

My Reward:

Today's Self-Care
(Non-Negotiable)

Daily Task List

Priority Tasks
1.
2.
3.
Bonus Tasks
1.
2.
3.
Tasks to Delegate
1.
2.
3.

Today's Cash Flow

Cash In	Cash Out

Total In _____   Total Out _____

Daily Health Check
(How did I exercise my body for at least 30 minutes today? How will I do it tomorrow?)

Today's Lessons
(What did I learn today?)

1.
2.
3.

Today's Dominate Emotion
(Do I want to repeat this emotion or doesit need to improve?)

Emotion:

Why?:

Keep or Improve:

Today's Blessings
(Today I am grateful for:)

1.
2.
3.

Today's Scripture:	
Today's Affirmation:	

Wake-Up Routine

- ☐ Warm Water + Lemon
- ☐ Pray
- ☐ Exercise
- ☐ _____

- ☐ Meditate
- ☐ Affirm
- ☐ Express Love
- ☐ _____

Daily Schedule and Assessment

(In the Assessment column, write down if the actual activity that occurred was useful, wasteful or if the jury's still out.)

	Scheduled	Adjustments	Assessment
4AM			
5 AM			
6 AM			
7 AM			
8 AM			
9 AM			
10 AM			
11 AM			
12 PM			
1 PM			
2 PM			
3 PM			
4 PM			
5 PM			
6 PM			
7 PM			
8 PM			
9 PM			
10 PM			
11 PM			
12 AM			
1 AM			
2 AM			
3 AM			

Wind-Down Routine

- ☐ Reflect
- ☐ Plan
- ☐ Pray
- ☐ _____

- ☐ Give Thanks
- ☐ Ask
- ☐ Release
- ☐ _____

Journaling: Wind-Down Reflections

- Who did I help today and how?

_____

_____

_____

_____

- Who helped me today and how?

_____

_____

_____

_____

- What do I want to remember most about today?

_____

_____

_____

_____

- What do I want tomorrow to bring?

_____

_____

_____

_____

Rainmaking Relationships

People to Contact Today	Thank You Notes to Send Today

Daily Reflections

Day: _____   Date: _____

Win Every Day!
(Write down today's top objective.)

Goal:

My Reward:

Today's Self-Care
(Non-Negotiable)

Daily Task List

Priority Tasks
1.
2.
3.
Bonus Tasks
1.
2.
3.
Tasks to Delegate
1.
2.
3.

Today's Cash Flow

Cash In	Cash Out

Total In _____   Total Out _____

Daily Health Check
(How did I exercise my body for at least 30 minutes today? How will I do it tomorrow?)

Today's Lessons
(What did I learn today?)

1.
2.
3.

Today's Dominate Emotion
(Do I want to repeat this emotion or doesit need to improve?)

Emotion:

Why?:

Keep or Improve:

Today's Blessings
(Today I am grateful for:)

1.
2.
3.

Today's Scripture:	

Today's Affirmation:	

Wake-Up Routine

☐	Warm Water + Lemon	☐	Meditate
☐	Pray	☐	Affirm
☐	Exercise	☐	Express Love
☐	_____	☐	_____

Daily Schedule and Assessment
(In the Assessment column, write down if the actual activity that occurred was useful, wasteful or if the jury's still out.)

	Scheduled	Adjustments	Assessment
4AM			
5 AM			
6 AM			
7 AM			
8 AM			
9 AM			
10 AM			
11 AM			
12 PM			
1 PM			
2 PM			
3 PM			
4 PM			
5 PM			
6 PM			
7 PM			
8 PM			
9 PM			
10 PM			
11 PM			
12 AM			
1 AM			
2 AM			
3 AM			

Wind-Down Routine

☐	Reflect	☐	Give Thanks
☐	Plan	☐	Ask
☐	Pray	☐	Release
☐	_____	☐	_____

Journaling: Wind-Down Reflections

- Who did I help today and how?

_____

_____

_____

_____

- Who helped me today and how?

_____

_____

_____

_____

- What do I want to remember most about today?

_____

_____

_____

_____

- What do I want tomorrow to bring?

_____

_____

_____

_____

Rainmaking Relationships

People to Contact Today

Thank You Notes to Send Today

Daily Reflections

Day: _____   Date: _____

Win Every Day!
(Write down today's top objective.)

Goal:

My Reward:

Today's Self-Care
(Non-Negotiable)

Daily Task List

Priority Tasks
1.
2.
3.
Bonus Tasks
1.
2.
3.
Tasks to Delegate
1.
2.
3.

Today's Cash Flow

Cash In	Cash Out
Total In _____	Total Out _____

Daily Health Check
(How did I exercise my body for at least 30 minutes today? How will I do it tomorrow?)

Today's Lessons
(What did I learn today?)

1.
2.
3.

Today's Dominate Emotion
(Do I want to repeat this emotion or doesit need to improve?)

Emotion:

Why?:

Keep or Improve:

Today's Blessings
(Today I am grateful for:)

1.
2.
3.

	Today's Scripture:	

	Today's Affirmation:	

Wake-Up Routine

☐ Warm Water + Lemon   ☐ Meditate
☐ Pray   ☐ Affirm
☐ Exercise   ☐ Express Love
☐ _____   ☐ _____

Daily Schedule and Assessment
(In the Assessment column, write down if the actual activity that occurred was useful, wasteful or if the jury's still out.)

	Scheduled	Adjustments	Assessment
4AM			
5 AM			
6 AM			
7 AM			
8 AM			
9 AM			
10 AM			
11 AM			
12 PM			
1 PM			
2 PM			
3 PM			
4 PM			
5 PM			
6 PM			
7 PM			
8 PM			
9 PM			
10 PM			
11 PM			
12 AM			
1 AM			
2 AM			
3 AM			

Wind-Down Routine

☐ Reflect   ☐ Give Thanks
☐ Plan   ☐ Ask
☐ Pray   ☐ Release
☐ _____   ☐ _____

Journaling: Wind-Down Reflections

- Who did I help today and how?

_____

_____

_____

_____

- Who helped me today and how?

_____

_____

_____

_____

- What do I want to remember most about today?

_____

_____

_____

_____

- What do I want tomorrow to bring?

_____

_____

_____

_____

Rainmaking Relationships

People to Contact Today

Thank You Notes to Send Today

Daily Reflections

Day: _____   Date: _____

Win Every Day!
(Write down today's top objective.)

Goal:

My Reward:

Today's Self-Care
(Non-Negotiable)

Daily Task List

Priority Tasks
1.
2.
3.
Bonus Tasks
1.
2.
3.
Tasks to Delegate
1.
2.
3.

Today's Cash Flow

Cash In	Cash Out

Total In _____   Total Out _____

Daily Health Check
(How did I exercise my body for at least 30 minutes today? How will I do it tomorrow?)

Today's Lessons
(What did I learn today?)

1.
2.
3.

Today's Dominate Emotion
(Do I want to repeat this emotion or doesit need to improve?)

Emotion:

Why?:

Keep or Improve:

Today's Blessings
(Today I am grateful for:)

1.
2.
3.

Today's Scripture:	

Today's Affirmation:	

Wake-Up Routine

☐	Warm Water + Lemon	☐	Meditate
☐	Pray	☐	Affirm
☐	Exercise	☐	Express Love
☐	_____	☐	_____

Daily Schedule and Assessment

(In the Assessment column, write down if the actual activity that occurred was useful, wasteful or if the jury's still out.)

	Scheduled	Adjustments	Assessment
4AM			
5 AM			
6 AM			
7 AM			
8 AM			
9 AM			
10 AM			
11 AM			
12 PM			
1 PM			
2 PM			
3 PM			
4 PM			
5 PM			
6 PM			
7 PM			
8 PM			
9 PM			
10 PM			
11 PM			
12 AM			
1 AM			
2 AM			
3 AM			

Wind-Down Routine

☐	Reflect	☐	Give Thanks
☐	Plan	☐	Ask
☐	Pray	☐	Release
☐	_____	☐	_____

Journaling: Wind-Down Reflections

- Who did I help today and how?

_____

_____

_____

_____

- Who helped me today and how?

_____

_____

_____

_____

- What do I want to remember most about today?

_____

_____

_____

_____

- What do I want tomorrow to bring?

_____

_____

_____

_____

Rainmaking Relationships

People to Contact Today	Thank You Notes to Send Today

Daily Reflections

Day: _____   Date: _____

Win Every Day!
(Write down today's top objective.)

Goal:

My Reward:

Today's Self-Care
(Non-Negotiable)

Daily Task List

Priority Tasks
1.
2.
3.
Bonus Tasks
1.
2.
3.
Tasks to Delegate
1.
2.
3.

Today's Cash Flow

Cash In	Cash Out
Total In _____	Total Out _____

Daily Health Check
(How did I exercise my body for at least 30 minutes today? How will I do it tomorrow?)

Today's Lessons
(What did I learn today?)

1.
2.
3.

Today's Dominate Emotion
(Do I want to repeat this emotion or doesit need to improve?)

Emotion:

Why?:

Keep or Improve:

Today's Blessings
(Today I am grateful for:)

1.
2.
3.

Today's Scripture:	
Today's Affirmation:	

Wake-Up Routine

☐	Warm Water + Lemon	☐	Meditate
☐	Pray	☐	Affirm
☐	Exercise	☐	Express Love
☐	_____	☐	_____

Daily Schedule and Assessment
(In the Assessment column, write down if the actual activity that occurred was useful, wasteful or if the jury's still out.)

	Scheduled	Adjustments	Assessment
4AM			
5 AM			
6 AM			
7 AM			
8 AM			
9 AM			
10 AM			
11 AM			
12 PM			
1 PM			
2 PM			
3 PM			
4 PM			
5 PM			
6 PM			
7 PM			
8 PM			
9 PM			
10 PM			
11 PM			
12 AM			
1 AM			
2 AM			
3 AM			

Wind-Down Routine

☐	Reflect	☐	Give Thanks
☐	Plan	☐	Ask
☐	Pray	☐	Release
☐	_____	☐	_____

Journaling: Wind-Down Reflections

- Who did I help today and how?

_____

_____

_____

_____

- Who helped me today and how?

_____

_____

_____

_____

- What do I want to remember most about today?

_____

_____

_____

_____

- What do I want tomorrow to bring?

_____

_____

_____

_____

Rainmaking Relationships

People to Contact Today	Thank You Notes to Send Today

Daily Reflections

Day: _____ Date: _____

Win Every Day!
(Write down today's top objective.)

Goal:

My Reward:

Today's Self-Care
(Non-Negotiable)

Daily Task List

Priority Tasks
1.
2.
3.
Bonus Tasks
1.
2.
3.
Tasks to Delegate
1.
2.
3.

Today's Cash Flow

Cash In	Cash Out
Total In _____	Total Out _____

Daily Health Check
(How did I exercise my body for at least 30 minutes today? How will I do it tomorrow?)

Today's Lessons
(What did I learn today?)

1.
2.
3.

Today's Dominate Emotion
(Do I want to repeat this emotion or doesit need to improve?)

Emotion:

Why?:

Keep or Improve:

Today's Blessings
(Today I am grateful for:)

1.
2.
3.

Today's Scripture:	

Today's Affirmation:	

Wake-Up Routine

☐	Warm Water + Lemon	☐	Meditate	
☐	Pray	☐	Affirm	
☐	Exercise	☐	Express Love	
☐	_____	☐	_____	

Daily Schedule and Assessment

(In the Assessment column, write down if the actual activity that occurred was useful, wasteful or if the jury's still out.)

	Scheduled	Adjustments	Assessment
4AM			
5 AM			
6 AM			
7 AM			
8 AM			
9 AM			
10 AM			
11 AM			
12 PM			
1 PM			
2 PM			
3 PM			
4 PM			
5 PM			
6 PM			
7 PM			
8 PM			
9 PM			
10 PM			
11 PM			
12 AM			
1 AM			
2 AM			
3 AM			

Wind-Down Routine

☐	Reflect	☐	Give Thanks	
☐	Plan	☐	Ask	
☐	Pray	☐	Release	
☐	_____	☐	_____	

Journaling: Wind-Down Reflections

- Who did I help today and how?

_____

_____

_____

_____

- Who helped me today and how?

_____

_____

_____

_____

- What do I want to remember most about today?

_____

_____

_____

_____

- What do I want tomorrow to bring?

_____

_____

_____

_____

Rainmaking Relationships

People to Contact Today

Thank You Notes to Send Today

Daily Reflections

Day: _____   Date: _____

Win Every Day!
(Write down today's top objective.)

Goal:

My Reward:

Today's Self-Care
(Non-Negotiable)

Daily Task List

Priority Tasks
1.
2.
3.
Bonus Tasks
1.
2.
3.
Tasks to Delegate
1.
2.
3.

Today's Cash Flow

Cash In	Cash Out

Total In _____   Total Out _____

Daily Health Check
(How did I exercise my body for at least 30 minutes today? How will I do it tomorrow?)

Today's Lessons
(What did I learn today?)

1.
2.
3.

Today's Dominate Emotion
(Do I want to repeat this emotion or does it need to improve?)

Emotion:

Why?:

Keep or Improve:

Today's Blessings
(Today I am grateful for:)

1.
2.
3.

Today's Scripture:	

Today's Affirmation:	

Wake-Up Routine

☐	Warm Water + Lemon	☐	Meditate
☐	Pray	☐	Affirm
☐	Exercise	☐	Express Love
☐	_____	☐	_____

Daily Schedule and Assessment
(In the Assessment column, write down if the actual activity that occurred was useful, wasteful or if the jury's still out.)

	Scheduled	Adjustments	Assessment
4AM			
5 AM			
6 AM			
7 AM			
8 AM			
9 AM			
10 AM			
11 AM			
12 PM			
1 PM			
2 PM			
3 PM			
4 PM			
5 PM			
6 PM			
7 PM			
8 PM			
9 PM			
10 PM			
11 PM			
12 AM			
1 AM			
2 AM			
3 AM			

Wind-Down Routine

☐	Reflect	☐	Give Thanks
☐	Plan	☐	Ask
☐	Pray	☐	Release
☐	_____	☐	_____

Journaling: Wind-Down Reflections

- Who did I help today and how?

_____

_____

_____

_____

- Who helped me today and how?

_____

_____

_____

_____

- What do I want to remember most about today?

_____

_____

_____

_____

- What do I want tomorrow to bring?

_____

_____

_____

_____

Rainmaking Relationships

People to Contact Today	Thank You Notes to Send Today

Daily Reflections

Day: _____   Date: _____

Win Every Day!
(Write down today's top objective.)

Goal:

My Reward:

Today's Self-Care
(Non-Negotiable)

Daily Task List

Priority Tasks
1.
2.
3.
Bonus Tasks
1.
2.
3.
Tasks to Delegate
1.
2.
3.

Today's Cash Flow

Cash In	Cash Out
Total In _____	Total Out _____

Daily Health Check
(How did I exercise my body for at least 30 minutes today? How will I do it tomorrow?)

Today's Lessons
(What did I learn today?)

1.
2.
3.

Today's Dominate Emotion
(Do I want to repeat this emotion or doesit need to improve?)

Emotion:

Why?:

Keep or Improve:

Today's Blessings
(Today I am grateful for:)

1.
2.
3.

Today's Scripture:	

Today's Affirmation:	

Wake-Up Routine

☐ Warm Water + Lemon   ☐ Meditate
☐ Pray   ☐ Affirm
☐ Exercise   ☐ Express Love
☐ _____   ☐ _____

Daily Schedule and Assessment
(In the Assessment column, write down if the actual activity that occurred was useful, wasteful or if the jury's still out.)

	Scheduled	Adjustments	Assessment
4AM			
5 AM			
6 AM			
7 AM			
8 AM			
9 AM			
10 AM			
11 AM			
12 PM			
1 PM			
2 PM			
3 PM			
4 PM			
5 PM			
6 PM			
7 PM			
8 PM			
9 PM			
10 PM			
11 PM			
12 AM			
1 AM			
2 AM			
3 AM			

Wind-Down Routine

☐ Reflect   ☐ Give Thanks
☐ Plan   ☐ Ask
☐ Pray   ☐ Release
☐ _____   ☐ _____

Journaling: Wind-Down Reflections

- Who did I help today and how?

_____

_____

_____

_____

- Who helped me today and how?

_____

_____

_____

_____

- What do I want to remember most about today?

_____

_____

_____

_____

- What do I want tomorrow to bring?

_____

_____

_____

_____

Rainmaking Relationships

People to Contact Today	Thank You Notes to Send Today

Daily Reflections

Day: _____   Date: _____

Win Every Day!
(Write down today's top objective.)

Goal:

My Reward:

Today's Self-Care
(Non-Negotiable)

Daily Task List

Priority Tasks
1.
2.
3.
Bonus Tasks
1.
2.
3.
Tasks to Delegate
1.
2.
3.

Today's Cash Flow

Cash In	Cash Out
Total In _____	Total Out _____

Daily Health Check
(How did I exercise my body for at least 30 minutes today? How will I do it tomorrow?)

Today's Lessons
(What did I learn today?)

1.
2.
3.

Today's Dominate Emotion
(Do I want to repeat this emotion or doesit need to improve?)

Emotion:

Why?:

Keep or Improve:

Today's Blessings
(Today I am grateful for:)

1.
2.
3.

Today's Scripture:	
Today's Affirmation:	

Wake-Up Routine

☐	Warm Water + Lemon	☐	Meditate
☐	Pray	☐	Affirm
☐	Exercise	☐	Express Love
☐	_____	☐	_____

Daily Schedule and Assessment
(In the Assessment column, write down if the actual activity that occurred was useful, wasteful or if the jury's still out.)

	Scheduled	Adjustments	Assessment
4AM			
5 AM			
6 AM			
7 AM			
8 AM			
9 AM			
10 AM			
11 AM			
12 PM			
1 PM			
2 PM			
3 PM			
4 PM			
5 PM			
6 PM			
7 PM			
8 PM			
9 PM			
10 PM			
11 PM			
12 AM			
1 AM			
2 AM			
3 AM			

Wind-Down Routine

☐	Reflect	☐	Give Thanks
☐	Plan	☐	Ask
☐	Pray	☐	Release
☐	_____	☐	_____

Journaling: Wind-Down Reflections

- Who did I help today and how?

_____

_____

_____

_____

- Who helped me today and how?

_____

_____

_____

_____

- What do I want to remember most about today?

_____

_____

_____

_____

- What do I want tomorrow to bring?

_____

_____

_____

_____

Rainmaking Relationships

People to Contact Today	Thank You Notes to Send Today

Daily Reflections

Day: _____   Date: _____

Win Every Day!
(Write down today's top objective.)

Goal:

My Reward:

Today's Self-Care
(Non-Negotiable)

Daily Task List

Priority Tasks
1.
2.
3.
Bonus Tasks
1.
2.
3.
Tasks to Delegate
1.
2.
3.

Today's Cash Flow

Cash In	Cash Out
Total In _____	Total Out _____

Daily Health Check
(How did I exercise my body for at least 30 minutes today? How will I do it tomorrow?)

Today's Lessons
(What did I learn today?)

1.
2.
3.

Today's Dominate Emotion
(Do I want to repeat this emotion or doesit need to improve?)

Emotion:

Why?:

Keep or Improve:

Today's Blessings
(Today I am grateful for:)

1.
2.
3.

Today's Scripture:	

Today's Affirmation:	

Wake-Up Routine

☐	Warm Water + Lemon	☐	Meditate
☐	Pray	☐	Affirm
☐	Exercise	☐	Express Love
☐	_____	☐	_____

Daily Schedule and Assessment
(In the Assessment column, write down if the actual activity that occurred was useful, wasteful or if the jury's still out.)

	Scheduled	Adjustments	Assessment
4AM			
5 AM			
6 AM			
7 AM			
8 AM			
9 AM			
10 AM			
11 AM			
12 PM			
1 PM			
2 PM			
3 PM			
4 PM			
5 PM			
6 PM			
7 PM			
8 PM			
9 PM			
10 PM			
11 PM			
12 AM			
1 AM			
2 AM			
3 AM			

Wind-Down Routine

☐	Reflect	☐	Give Thanks
☐	Plan	☐	Ask
☐	Pray	☐	Release
☐	_____	☐	_____

Journaling: Wind-Down Reflections

- Who did I help today and how?

_____

_____

_____

_____

- Who helped me today and how?

_____

_____

_____

_____

- What do I want to remember most about today?

_____

_____

_____

_____

- What do I want tomorrow to bring?

_____

_____

_____

_____

Rainmaking Relationships

People to Contact Today

Thank You Notes to Send Today

Daily Reflections

Day: _____   Date: _____

Win Every Day!
(Write down today's top objective.)

Goal:

My Reward:

Today's Self-Care
(Non-Negotiable)

Daily Task List

Priority Tasks
1.
2.
3.
Bonus Tasks
1.
2.
3.
Tasks to Delegate
1.
2.
3.

Today's Cash Flow

Cash In	Cash Out

Total In _____   Total Out _____

Daily Health Check
(How did I exercise my body for at least 30 minutes today? How will I do it tomorrow?)

Today's Lessons
(What did I learn today?)

1.
2.
3.

Today's Dominate Emotion
(Do I want to repeat this emotion or doesit need to improve?)

Emotion:

Why?:

Keep or Improve:

Today's Blessings
(Today I am grateful for:)

1.
2.
3.

© 2016 UpwardAction LLC
www.FaithFocusFlow.com

	Today's Scripture:	
	Today's Scripture:	
	Today's Affirmation:	

Wake-Up Routine

☐	Warm Water + Lemon	☐	Meditate
☐	Pray	☐	Affirm
☐	Exercise	☐	Express Love
☐	_____	☐	_____

Daily Schedule and Assessment
(In the Assessment column, write down if the actual activity that occurred was useful, wasteful or if the jury's still out.)

	Scheduled	Adjustments	Assessment
4AM			
5 AM			
6 AM			
7 AM			
8 AM			
9 AM			
10 AM			
11 AM			
12 PM			
1 PM			
2 PM			
3 PM			
4 PM			
5 PM			
6 PM			
7 PM			
8 PM			
9 PM			
10 PM			
11 PM			
12 AM			
1 AM			
2 AM			
3 AM			

Wind-Down Routine

☐	Reflect	☐	Give Thanks
☐	Plan	☐	Ask
☐	Pray	☐	Release
☐	_____	☐	_____

Journaling: Wind-Down Reflections

- Who did I help today and how?

_____

_____

_____

_____

- Who helped me today and how?

_____

_____

_____

_____

- What do I want to remember most about today?

_____

_____

_____

_____

- What do I want tomorrow to bring?

_____

_____

_____

_____

Rainmaking Relationships

People to Contact Today

Thank You Notes to Send Today

Daily Reflections

Thank you for investing in
**A S.M.A.R.T. Goal Daily Planner
for Business and Life**.

Connect with us on social media and let us know how this planner helped to transform your life and business.

We also want to know how we can make the 2nd edition better.

You can find us on Facebook, Twitter, Instagram, Periscope, Pinterest and LinkedIn by searching for
@UpwardAction.

Blessings!
Team UpwardAction®

Visit us online at
www.FaithFocusFlow.com
to receive special discounts for
re-orders of this planner and other
Faith.Focus.Flow. products.

Your receipt is required to
receive the discounts.